creative crafts from
plastic cups

By Nikki Connor
Illustrated by Sarah-Jane Neaves

Copper Beech Books
Brookfield, Connecticut

© Aladdin Books Ltd 1996
Designed and produced by
Aladdin Books Ltd
28 Percy Street
London W1P 0LD

First published in the United States
in 1996 by
Copper Beech Books,
an imprint of
The Millbrook Press
2 Old New Milford Road
Brookfield, Connecticut 06804

Design David West Children's Book
Design
Illustrator Sarah-Jane Neaves
Photographer Roger Vlitos

Printed in Belgium

Library of Congress Cataloging-in-
Publication Data

Connor, Nikki Plastic Cups / by Nikki
Connor : illustrated by Sarah-Jane
Neaves. p. cm. -- (Creative crafts from)
Summary: Provides
instructions for a variety of craft projects
for young children using plastic cups.
ISBN 0-7613-0539-4 (lib. bdg.). --
ISBN 0-7613-0514-9 (pbk.)
1. Plastic craft--Juvenile literature.
2. Drinking cups--Juvenile literature.
[1. Plastic craft. 2. Handicraft.]
I. Neaves, Sarah-Jane, ill. II. Title. III. Series.
TT297.C58   1996   96-12632
745.57'2--dc20   CIP AC

Contents

Before you start

A "what you need" ingredients panel appears with the photograph of each project. Decide which project you are going to make and collect everything you need.

The red, yellow, and blue paint cups mean that you need poster paints. All colors (except white) can be made by mixing together a combination of these three. See the color chart at the back of this book to find out how. You may choose instead to use ready mixed colors if you have them.

Use a pencil point to punch holes in paper or thin card. For holes in thicker cardboard and in plastic, use scissors – <u>adult help is needed for this</u>.

A dotted line in the instructions means you are to fold, not cut. A solid line shows where to cut.

Only use scissors that are especially designed for children's crafts. They usually have rounded ends. Always have an adult with you when you use them.

Where a project needs colored paper remember you may use any color you choose. If you have none, use white paper and paint it!

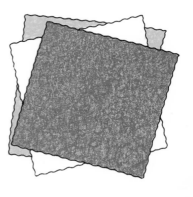

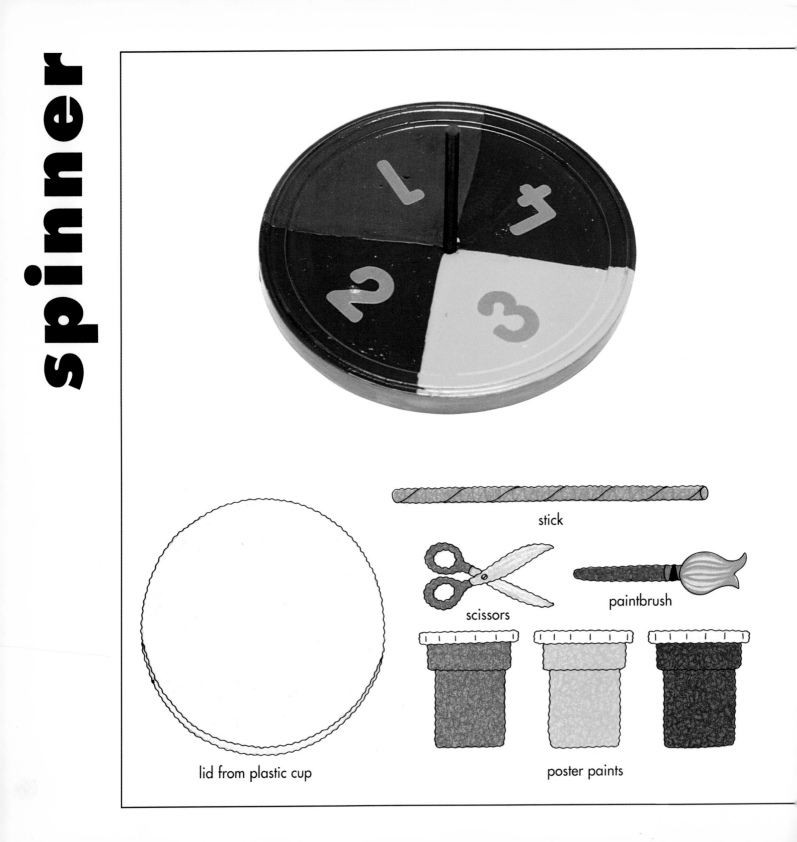

spinner

stick

scissors

paintbrush

lid from plastic cup

poster paints

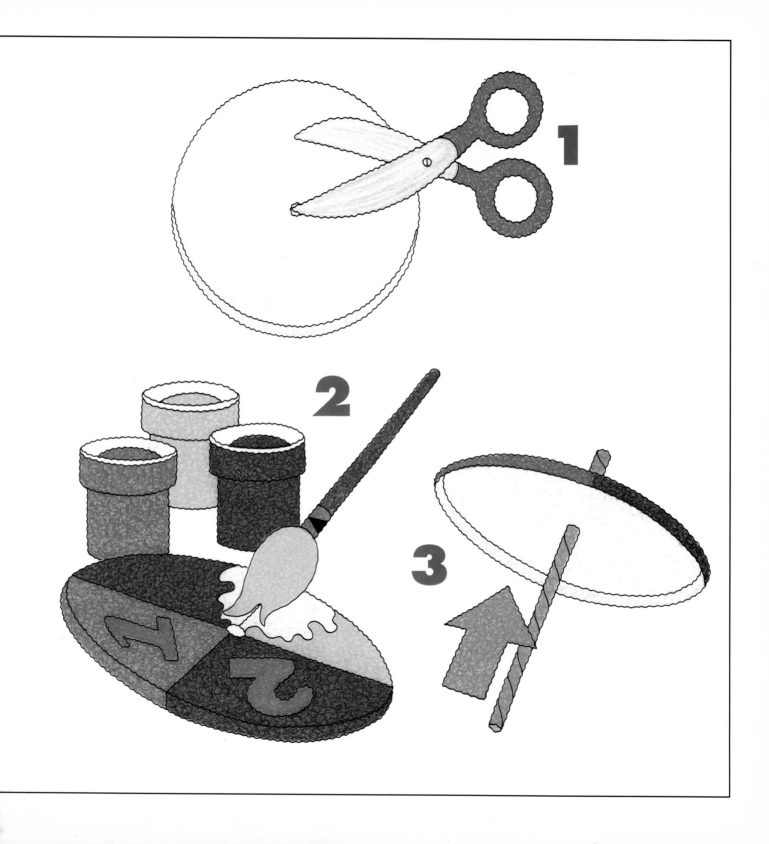

cup and ball

stick

bead

scissors

adhesive tape

plastic cup

string

paintbrush

poster paints

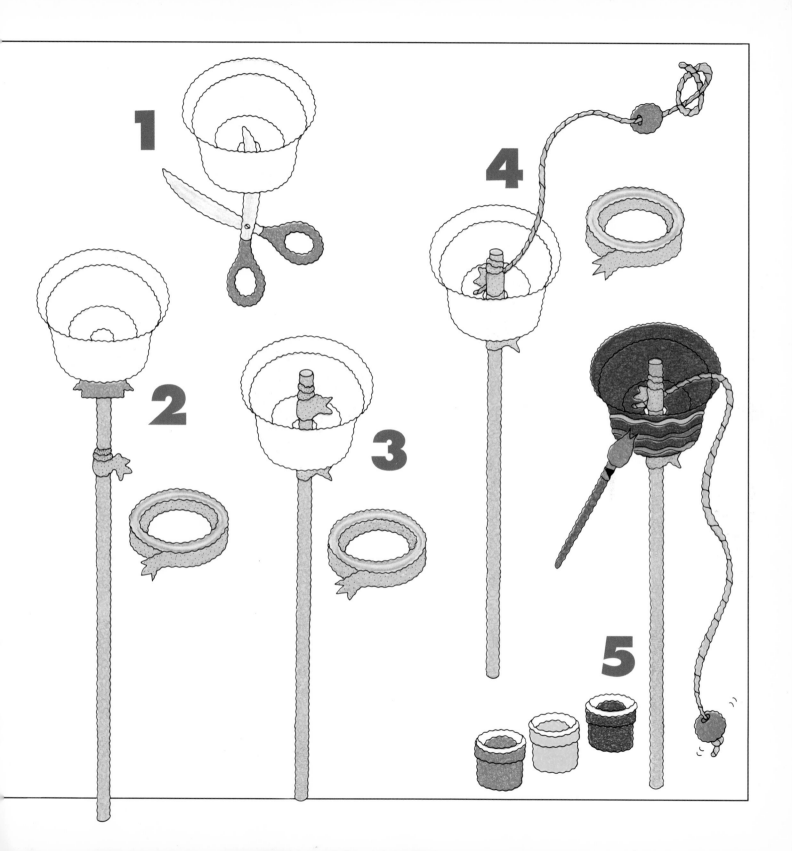

telephones

plastic cups

paintbrush

poster paints

scissors

string

shakers

lentils or rice

adhesive tape

stick-on shapes

paintbrush

plastic cups

poster paints

wagon

string

sticks

straws

scissors

glue

rubber bands

paper

plastic tub

plastic cups

adhesive tape

paintbrush

poster paints

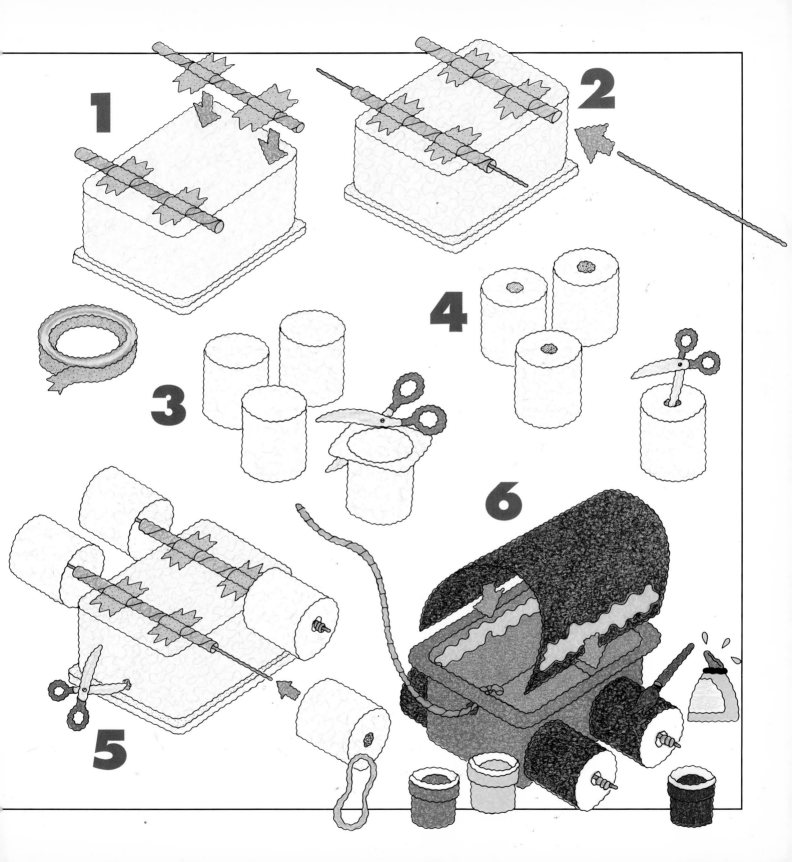

snake

stick

glue

plastic cups

paintbrush

colored paper

needle and thread

string

adhesive tape

scissors

poster paints

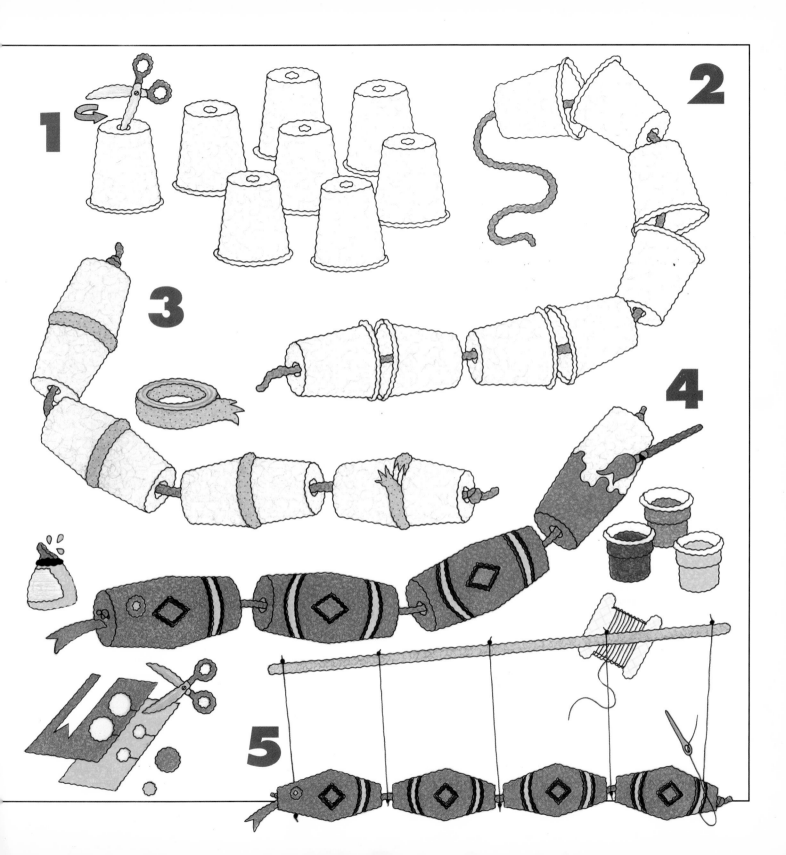

roll-a-ball

cardboard box

plastic cups

paper fastener

paper

marble

adhesive tape

glue

scissors

paintbrush

poster paints

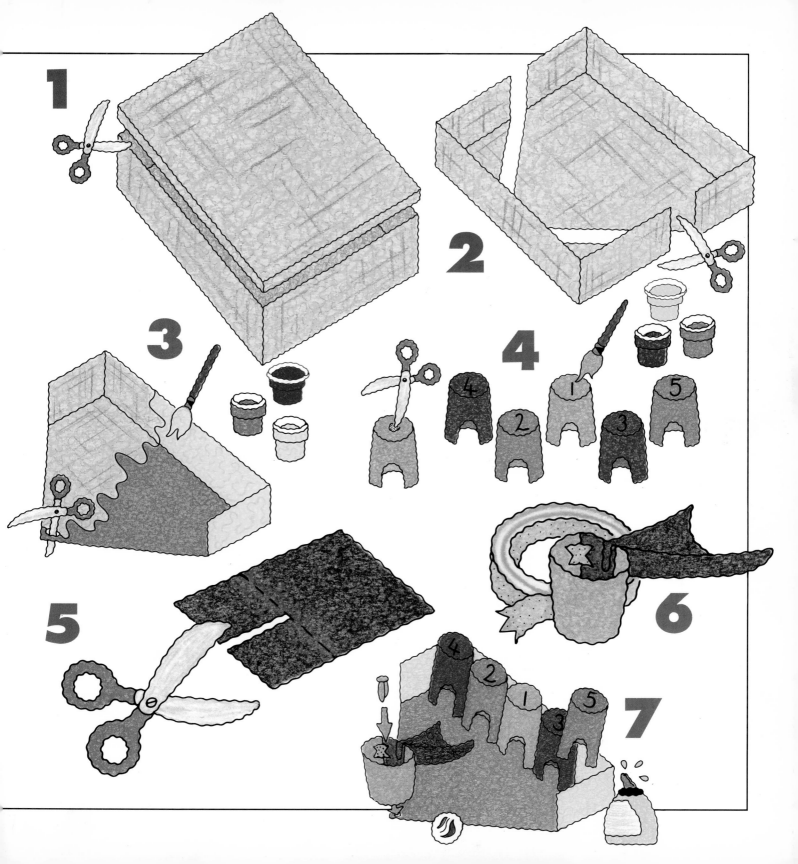

flowerpot

poster paints

glue

felt

stick

rubber band

scissors

plastic cup

paintbrush

drum

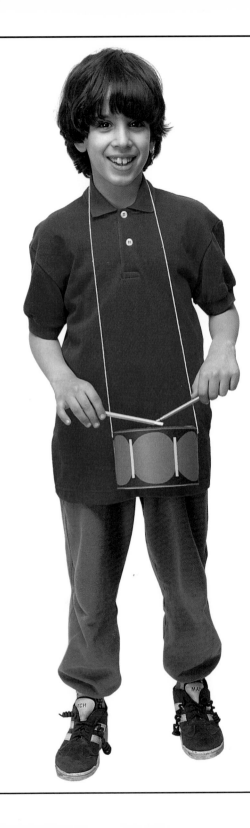

glue

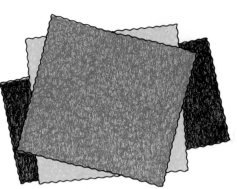

colored paper

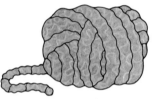

string

scissors

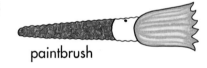

plastic cement

paintbrush

plastic tub

tissue paper

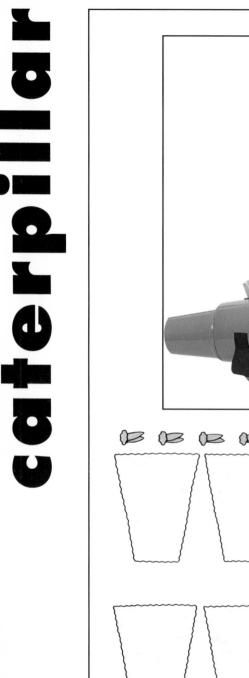

caterpillar

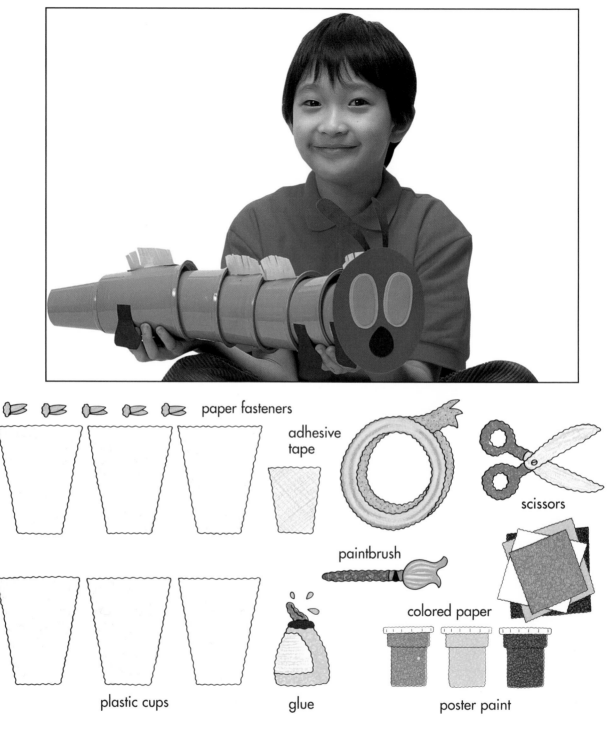

paper fasteners

adhesive tape

scissors

paintbrush

colored paper

plastic cups

glue

poster paint

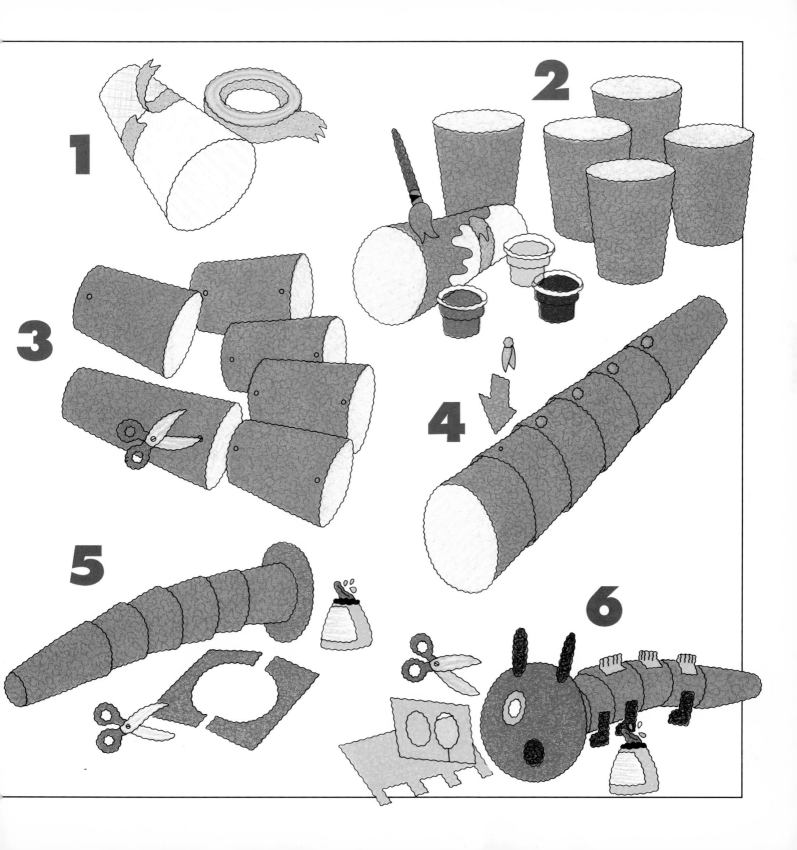

1

2

3

4

5

6

You can mix the three primary colors to make all the colors of the rainbow. Follow the chart below to mix the colors you want. The numbers on the cups show the proportions of each color you need to make the new color.

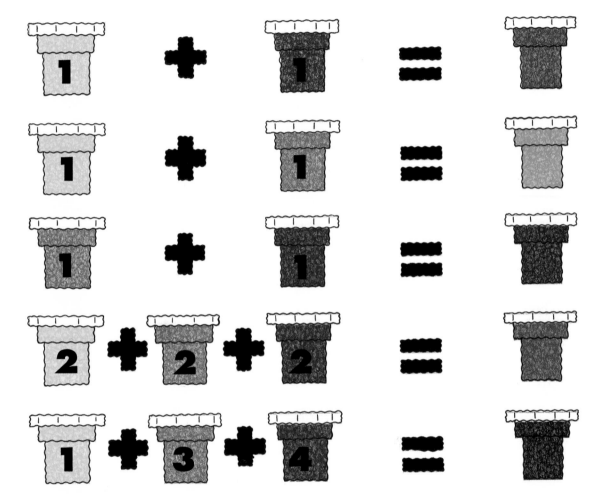

Different types of paint will give different results. Experiment by mixing different proportions of colors. Make sure you wash the brush before dipping it into each paint cup.